The Sermon on the Mount in Our Secular Age

The Sermon on the Mount in Our Secular Age

JESUS' SERMON FOR ALL SEASONS

Douglas D. Webster

REGENT COLLEGE PUBLISHING
Vancouver, British Columbia

The Sermon on the Mount in Our Secular Age
Copyright © 2020 Douglas D. Webster

Regent College Publishing
5800 University Boulevard
Vancouver, BC V6T 2E4 Canada

Regent College Publishing is an imprint of the Regent Bookstore (RegentBookstore.com). Views expressed in works published by Regent College Publishing are those of the author and do not necessarily represent the official position of Regent College (Regent-College.edu).

ISBN: 978-1-57383-580-0

THE SERMON ON THE MOUNT is the sum and substance of the Jesus way. The Sermon lays out what it means to take up the easy yoke and learn from him (Matthew 11:29). It is the definition of the great commandment to love God with our whole being and our neighbor as ourselves (Matthew 22:37-39). It is the content of the great commission "to teach all that I have commanded" (Matthew 28:19-20). The Sermon incarnates the vision of the abundant life (John 10:10). It embodies the essence of the renewed mind (Romans 12:1-2) and the new creation (2 Corinthians 5:17). It envisions what it means to fix our eyes on Jesus (Hebrews 12:1) and demonstrates the reality of the new self (Ephesians 4:20-24). Jesus gave the sermon with Jeremiah's prophecy in mind: "I will put my law in their minds and write it on their hearts" (Jeremiah 31:33). To obey the words of Jesus is to bind ourselves to the Lord in an "everlasting covenant" (Jeremiah 50:5).

The followers of Jesus Christ turn to the Sermon on the Mount to understand what it means to be in Christ regardless of their cultural background. In three concise, compact chapters, Matthew captures Jesus' Kingdom ethic, along with the gospel's revelatory authority, covenant community, and historical destiny. The Sermon conveys in practical, down-to-earth, terms what it means to live into the gospel of grace for the people of God whether they are from Nigeria or Brazil or Canada. Believers from all over the world meet around the Sermon on the Mount to learn what it means to take up our cross and follow Jesus.

Matthew 5-7 has been my go-to-text for discipleship training in Ulan Batar, Mongolia, Bloomington, Indiana, Denver, Colorado, San Diego, California, Phnom Penh, Cambodia, Toronto, Canada, New York, New York, and Birmingham, Alabama. The Sermon is Jesus' cross-cultural manifesto relating his gospel to all people, all ethnic groups, all races, all locations, all religions, and all social classes. The Sermon on the Mount is a gift that does justice to both the Christ follower's internal character and external action, to the mission of the church and the need for missions, to the individual person and to the body-and-soul-in-community, and to the present as well as the future.

The Sermon on the Mount is necessary for all believers, because it brings clarity and understanding to what it means to follow Jesus. Many sincere, well-intentioned believers have been frustrated, manipulated, and led astray by forms of Christianity that ignore the clear teaching of Jesus. In the effort to make Christianity more appealing and easier to accept, we have inadvertently made it more difficult. People wonderfully saved by the grace of Christ are swept up into religious practices, moralistic pressures, and ethical positions that rob them of the joy of following the Lord Jesus. Their identity and priorities are confused. Their understanding of the nature of righteousness is skewed, and their life-goals have more to do with personal ambition than a passion for Christ. They are tired of predictable formulas for spiritual success that are no match for the harsh realities of living for Christ in their culture. The power of Christ's imputed righteousness sets them free to live under the law of Christ.

The Sermon is necessary spiritual direction for the hard work of disentangling "the life and identity of the church from the life and identity of American society." It also effectively "decouples" the public impact of the Christian life from political strategies."[1] Jesus gives us a high impact profile of the believer-in-community who is in the world but not of the world, "exercising a fundamentally different kind of social power."[2] The believer's cultural impact flows from humble dependence and inti-

---

1. James Davison Hunter, *To Change the World: The Irony, Tragedy, and Possibility of Christianity in the Late Modern World* (New York: Oxford University Press, 2010), 184.

2. Hunter, *To Change the World*, 188.

macy with the triune God, submission to the will of God, a sacrificial compassion for others, a rejection of worldly strategies of status and privilege, and a commitment to the gospel of Jesus Christ that is meant for all people.

Jesus describes beatitude-based believers who have salt and light impact in a world that needs preservation and illumination. They demonstrate a righteousness that surpasses the righteousness of the religious. In Christ, their real-world, life-related social righteousness fulfills the law as God intended. Their good works shine before others in all the practical areas of life, love, marriage, truth, justice, and reconciliation. Their witness brings glory to the Father in heaven.

Their hidden, personal righteousness—their giving, praying, and fasting, is not to impress others but to be in communion with the heavenly Father. Jesus' five "do nots" free disciples from bondage to materialism, competing loyalties, idolatry, self-righteousness, and false guilt. Believers depend upon their Father in heaven in order to treat others the way they would like to be treated. Mutual benefit designed by the will of God sums up the Law and the Prophets.

Jesus weaves his conclusion with three either/or decisions. Disciples choose the narrow gate over the broad way. They identify false prophets as wolves dressed in sheep's clothing. They are bad fruit from bad trees. Impressive outward acts of piety do not fool the Lord and they must not fool his disciples. Jesus closes with a vivid like sheep without a shepherd" (Matthew 9:36). Against the backdrop of Galilean darkness, Jesus "went up on a mountainside and sat down" (Matthew 12:20).

The scene is reminiscent of Moses when he received the Law on Mount Sinai. But Matthew wants us to remember something more. Jesus has been introduced to us as "Immanuel"— God with us: worshiped by the Magi, baptized by John, and confirmed by the Spirit of God who declared, "This is my Son, whom I love; with him I am well pleased." One greater than Moses has come and he takes his seat to teach *publicly* with all humility and authority. In the midst of the darkness and the tragedy of the human condition, in calm composure and quiet reason, Jesus exemplifies gospel shalom. His open, non-anxious engagement with the world is a model for all who seek to proclaim the good news. The darkness may be intimidating but it is no excuse for those who share the gospel to express anger or fear.

Darkness is dark no matter what form it takes, but it is undoubtedly true that the post-Galilean darkness of the modern age is different in ways unknown to Jesus' first hearers. Many in the secular age find themselves "suspended between the malaise of immanence and the memory of transcendence." They are taught "to face the fact that the universe is without transcendent meaning, without eternal purpose, without supernatural significance."[1] Exclusive humanism and expressive individualism are heralded as the only real options in an age that renegotiates the meaning of the person, society, human flourishing, time, and authenticity. Since many are convinced that life has no overarching purpose, the burden falls on the self to invent meaning and significance. The quest for meaning has eclipsed the quest for salvation. The fear facing people today is not the wrath of God so much as "a terrifying emptiness, a kind of vertigo, or even a fracturing of our world. . . . Making sense of our life is the object of a quest."[2]

Today's "stripped down ontology" excludes transcendent meaning and pushes the burden onto the individual to invent and articulate meaning. The rising rate of suicide in the United States may reflect not only a mental health crisis but a metaphysical crisis. The suicides of Anthony Bourdain, Kate Spade, and Richard Russell (a seemingly much loved and befriended twenty-nine-year-old baggage handler at Seattle's Sea-Tac airport who described himself as "just a broken guy with a few screws loose"), underscore the burden of living in our own heads and the pressure to create meaning. Taylor writes, "A total and fully consistent subjectivism

1. James K. A. Smith, *How (Not) to Be Secular* (Grand Rapids, MI: Eerdmans, 2014), x, 77.

2. Charles Taylor, *Sources of the Self: The Making of the Modern Identity* (Cambridge, MA: Harvard University Press, 1992), 18.

would tend towards emptiness: nothing would count as a fulfillment in a world in which literally nothing was important but self-fulfillment."[3]

"God is dead. God remains dead. And we have killed him." Nietzsche proclaimed. "How shall we comfort ourselves. . . . What festivals of atonement, what sacred games shall we have to invent?"[4] The quest for meaning has become every person's right. Justice Anthony Kennedy said it plainly, "At the heart of liberty is the right to define one's own concept of existence, of meaning, of the universe, and of the mystery of human life." Professor Andrew Delbanco in *The Real American Dream* defines culture as the stories and symbols by which we try to hold back the melancholy suspicion that we live in a world without meaning.[5]

Christians, myself included, tend to be naive when it comes to following Jesus. We assume that a steady diet of church attendance, sermons, and Bible studies will overcome the pervasive impact of late-modern culture. But the evidence shows otherwise. The church in general appears evangelized by the world more than the world is evangelized by the church. Our priorities, con-

3. Taylor, *Sources of the Self*, 507.

4. Nietzsche, "The Gay Science," sec. 125, in *Basic Writings of Nietzsche*, trans. and ed. Walter Kaufmann (New York: The Modern Library, 2000).

5. Andrew Delbanco, *The Real American Dream: A Meditation on Hope* (Cambridge, MA: Harvard University Press, 1999), 23.

victions, passions, ambitions, and goals tend to reflect the prevailing culture more than the costly way of Jesus. We are conditioned by the values, norms, and ethos of the society-at-large in ways that seemingly evade our conscious awareness and intentional decision-making. The "soil" in which our lives take root is not the word of God and the Jesus way, but the secular culture. There is little "organic" connection in our daily lives to the gospel. The imperishable seed of the living and enduring word of God has fallen on rocky ground.

A deeply secular world has transformed American Christianity into its own image and believers seem powerless to resist. We ought to recognize, suggests Jamie Smith, how difficul it is for people shaped by the secular age to believe.[6] The Christian conception of truth is radical and the "buy in" is costly. Belief is founded on doctrines of Divine Creation, the Incarnation, the Redemption, the work of the Holy Spirit. Belief accepts as a description of fact, the Virgin Birth, the efficacy of Christ's atoning sacrifice, and life everlasting. We must not beguile unbelievers into thinking that Christianity is good because it builds self-esteem, strengthens marriages, offers comfort, and leads to success. Harry Blamires writes, "We have to insist that the Christian Faith is something solider, harder and tougher than even Christians like to think. Christianity is not a nice comforting

6. Smith, *How (Not) to Be Secular*, 6.

story that we make up as we go along, accommodating the demands of a harsh reality with the solace of a cherished reverie. It is not a cosy day-dream manufactured by each person more or less to suit his own taste. It is a matter of hard fact." Blamires continues, "We Christians appreciate its hardness just as much as those outside the Church. We are as fully aware of its difficulties as the outsiders are. We know that, in a sense, Christianity leaves us with an awful lot to swallow.... We must outdo the unbelievers in agreeing with them on that subject."[79]

I propose that we mount our resistance to cultural conformity by taking Jesus' Sermon on the Mount seriously. It is surprising that many of us who have identified ourselves as Christians for years remain semi-ignorant of Jesus' teaching. We are exposed to an eclectic background of spiritual snippets, ethical nuggets, and pious reflections, but we have not grasped the life-transforming impact of the gospel. We have not submitted to the Lord Jesus.

Although believers may have listened to sermons for years, many limit the Sermon on the Mount to the Beatitudes. Seldom do preachers preach beyond the beatitudes and when they do they tend to preach selectively from the rest of Matthew 5-7. It only takes about fifteen minutes to read the Sermon on the Mount slow-

7. Harry Blamires, *The Christian Mind* (London: SPCK, 1963), 120.

ly, but few believers grasp Jesus' complete and concise counter-cultural description of the Christian life in three chapters. G. K. Chesterton said, "On the first reading of the Sermon on the Mount you feel that it turns everything upside down, but the second time you read it you discover that it turns everything right side up. The first time you read it you feel that it is impossible, but the second time, you feel that nothing else is possible."[8]

8. E. Stanley Jones, *The Christ of the Mount: A Working Philosophy of Life* (London: Hodder and Stoughton, 1931), 14.

Beatitude-Based Believers

"Blessed are the poor in spirit, for theirs is the kingdom of heaven." (MATTHEW 5:3)

Jesus rejects the immanent frame and counters a Cartesian isolation of the self with a simple sentence. "Blessed are the poor in spirit, for theirs is the kingdom of heaven" (Matthew 5:3). "Blessed" and "kingdom" are code words for the transcendent reality that cannot be squeezed into an immanent frame. They cannot be reduced to, "Happy are those who believe in themselves for they will achieve their goals." or "Happy are those who are satisfied by life, who amuse themselves, who are content." Jesus begins with an understanding of happiness that cannot be found in the late modern "spiritual-nova, a kind of galloping pluralism on the spiritual plane."[1]

The gift of meaning is received as a given; its source is the living triune God. We would not be having this

1. Charles Taylor, *A Secular Age* (Cambridge, MA: Harvard University Press, 1918), 300.

conversation if that were not the case. There would be no blessing, no kingdom, and no one to depend upon. "The fear of the Lord is the beginning of wisdom, and knowledge of the Holy One is understanding" (Proverbs 9:10). Jesus drew on the Jewish roots of the word *blessed* (ashr) which means "to find the right path." "Blessed are those who find wisdom, those who gain understanding.... Her ways are pleasant ways, and all her paths are peace" (Proverbs 3:13, 17).

One of the four disciples listening to Jesus that day was John. It is intriguing to imagine John linking his initial experience of Jesus' teaching with his late-in-life vision of the scroll and the throne of God (Revelation 5:1-14). In The Revelation John describes being overwhelmed by the possibility that no one was worthy to open the scroll and reveal the consummation of salvation. He is overcome with sorrow as he contemplates the tragic possibility of the absence of revelation and the impossibility of redemption. John wept and wept because no one was found who was worthy to open the scroll.

This is the kind of weeping that Friedrich Nietzsche (1844-1900) despised, because he found such weeping to be an embarrassment to the human animal. For Nietzsche there never was a scroll to open; there is only the strong man and his will to power. Nietzsche drove skepticism and cynicism to its fatal and nihilistic conclusion. Nietzsche had the courage of his convictions, even if those convictions drove him mad. He sought "to think pessimism through to its depths and to liberate it" from Christianity, which he believed was an essentially cruel religion that asked people to sacrifice for nothing.[2]

The authority of the Lamb who was slain to open the scroll is one with the authority of Jesus to bless the poor in spirit and promise them the kingdom of heaven. Eight simple lines, known as the beatitudes, capture the essence of what it means to follow the crucified and risen Lord Jesus. The people of God are characterized by these eight fundamental emotional attitudes, these eight convictions of the soul, these eight character qualities of the inner person. Jesus paints a portrait of his disciples from the inside out. These beatitudes serve as a theology of conversion and a strategy for evangelism. They describe the Alpha and Omega of the Christian life. To be in Christ is to never graduate from the beatitudes. From the newest saint to the oldest believer, we see ourselves in the beatitudes.

The beatitudes are not a means of grace but a state of grace. They describe believers who by the grace of God know they are utterly dependent upon the Lord; they mourn for their sin and the sin of the world; they submit to the will of God; they hunger and thirst for righteousness; they show mercy because they have re-

2. Nietzsche, *Beyond Good and Evil*, sec. 56, 258.

ceived mercy; their passion for God is single-minded and whole-hearted; they are peacemakers; and they are persecuted because of righteousness.

The source of each of these beatitudes is rooted in the Old Testament. Their meaning is not determined by what the culture thinks of the poor, the meek, and the mournful. When Jesus gave the beatitudes he was preaching the Old Testament and his disciples understood them in the light of the Psalms and the Prophets.[3] If we were to examine the beatitudes from the perspective of our culture we might conclude that this is a tragic list of people who are down-and-out, lost causes, human lasts, who have no where to go but up. Some argue that Jesus announced God's grace to life's "hopeless cases," to the homeless, the unemployed, the disabled, the inner city child, the emotionally starved, the lonely, the incompetent, and the ignorant.[4] The world looks at this list and feels pity and sympathy and responds with a cliche, "But

3. The poor in spirt—Ps 34:6; 69:29,32; those who mourn—Isa 61:1-2; Ps 51:17; James 4:8-9; those who hunger and thirst—Ps 23:3; the merciful—Ps 86:3,6,16; 143:1; Micah 6:8; the pure in heart—Ps 24:5-6; the peacemakers—Ps 34:8, 14; James 3:18; those who are persecuted—1 Pet 2:12,16; 3:8-9.

4. Dallas Willard, *The Divine Conspiracy* (New York: Harper, 1998), 124.

by the grace of God go I." No one is so poor and miserable that they cannot be rescued by God's grace.

One commentator explained what led him to interpret the beatitudes as a list of "hopeless blessables" and "lost causes." A woman came to him after he had spoken on the beatitudes: "She told me her son had left the Christian faith because of the Beatitudes. He was a strong, intelligent man who had made the military his profession. As often happens, he had been told that the Beatitudes—with its list of the poor and the sad, the weak and the mild—were a picture of the ideal Christian. He explained to his mother simply: 'This is not me. I can never be like that.'"[5]

I doubt that the woman's son, a proud, self-confident warrior, would have been impressed by the words of Jesus: "I tell you the truth, unless you change and become like little children, you will never enter the kingdom of heaven" (Matthew 18:3). It is precisely at this point that the beatitudes must not be hijacked by the secular age as a repugnant profile of the messed up life. Jesus' message is counter-cultural to the core. *Each beatitude is a description of grace-shaped receptivity to the will of God.* This is what it means to have faith in Christ. The beatitudes are not a list of legalistic prerequisites or moralistic preconditions, but they are a description of the attitude of heart and the condition of the will that turns to

5. Willard, *The Divine Conspiracy*, 99.

God for blessing. The person who comes to God singing, "Just as I am without one plea," has not met a condition for acceptance as much as acknowledged his or her absolute need for God.

Jesus gave the beatitudes with the finality of the last word—the benediction. Yet this last word is also the first word. The Church ends and begins with his blessings. Each beatitude depends upon and contains all the other beatitudes. They are like the colors in a rainbow. They are derived from a single source of light—the Light of Christ, refracted into an array of distinguishable yet inseparable colors. His disciples are not meant to become anything more or less than beatitude-based believers. The beatitudes celebrate the life we have received by faith, not the life we have achieved by our effort. They remind us of God's work, not our performance. We never graduate from the beatitudes nor retire from their personal significance. They are a complete picture of the grace of Christ at work among the disciples. Charles Spurgeon warned, "Do not fall into the mistake of supposing that the opening verses of the Sermon on the Mount set forth how we are to be saved, or you may cause your soul to stumble. You will find the fullest light upon the matter of how to be saved in other parts of our Lord's teaching, but here He talks about the question, 'Who are the saved?'

or, 'What are the marks and evidences of a work of grace in the soul?'"[6]

6. Charles Spurgeon, *God Will Bless You* (New Kensington, PA: Whitaker House, 1998), 8.

Salt and Light Impact

"You are the salt of the earth. . . .You are the light of the world." (MATTHEW 5:13–14)

The impact of these embodied beatitudes reflects true personal transformation, authentic non-conformity to the world, a true alienation from the world (rather than an alien alienation), and a compelling form of evangelism. The seven-fold criteria for biblical resistance culminates in the eighth beatitude. The beatitudes are followed up and climaxed by two powerful *You Are* statements. "You are the salt of the earth. . . . You are the light of the world." These are statements of fact describing the followers of Jesus. Beatitude-based believers have God's kingdom, experience God's comfort, and will inherit God's earth. They have been blessed with God's righteousness and they are defined by God's mercy, vision, identity, and reward. What more could God give them? They have it all, and for that reason they *are* salt and light. "'You folks

are,' not 'You folks *ought* to be,' the most significant people on the planet."[1]

What it means to have salt and light impact is clar-
ified in Jesus' forthcoming explanation of heart righteousness. It is embodied in cruciform obedience and
reflected in the hidden righteousness of true spirituality.
But in every age, especially in the secular age, it is important to clarify that Jesus never promised to his disciples worldly success and political power. Jesus gives
no hint that faithful believers will change the world. He
never implies that his marginalized, persecuted followers will someday grab the reigns of power and wrestle
galloping pluralism into submission. Jesus has no vision
for Christians running the world, but he has every expectation of believers overcoming the world.

The Jesus way "moves in the opposite direction of
social theory," precisely because the strategies of the
world are understood and rejected.[2] Cultural change is
the complex product of elites, networks, technologies,
institutions, and ideas that interact in often volatile, un-
predictable ways.[3] For believers this top-down elitism
"is despicable and utterly anathema to the gospel they

---

1. Frederick Dale Bruner, *The Churchbook: Matthew,* 2 vols.
(Grand Rapids, MI: Eerdmans, 2004), 1:188.
2. Hunter, *To Change the World,* 95.
3. Hunter, *To Change the World,* 76, 92.

cherish."[4] The salt and light impact of deep Christian faith does little to offset the principalities and powers of this dark world. The gospel often invokes a retaliatory response from the enemy when it is effective.

Leslie Newbigin explains, "It follows that the visible embodiment of this new reality is not a movement which will take control of history and shape the future according to its own vision, not a new imperialism, not a victorious crusade. Its visible embodiment will be a community that lives by this story, a community whose existence is visibly defined in the regular rehearsing and reenactment of the story which has given it birth, the story of the self-emptying of God in the ministry, life, death, and resurrection of Jesus."[5] Old paganisms and the new messianisms fight against the Church with everything they have. Newbigin writes, "Wherever the gospel is preached, new ideologies appear—secular humanism, nationalism, Marxism—movements which offer the vision of new age, an age freed from all the ills that beset human life, freed from hunger and disease and war—on other terms.... Once the gospel is preached and there is a community which lives by the gospel, then the ques-

4. Hunter, *To Change the World*, 94.

5. Leslie Newbigin, *The Gospel in a Pluralist Society* (Grand Rapids, MI: Eerdmans, 1989), 120.

tion of the ultimate meaning of history is posed and other messiahs appear. So the crisis of history is deepened."[6]

So, let's be clear. When Jesus said, "You are the salt of the earth and the light of the world," he did not envision Christians taking over the world or taking back America or saving civilization. Jesus never implied such a grandiose strategy nor encouraged such naivete. It was never part of his plan. And believers who think it is are sadly beholden to the spirit of the age with its fascination with political ideology, consumerism, and individualism. Many believers who think they are fully committed followers of Jesus have no idea how much they are influenced by the world. They see themselves as world-changers but in reality they are worldly. Their veneer of cultural Christianity and pious optimism is no match for interacting with the culture. This is why we pay attention to Jesus' teaching on the meaning of being salt and light. His vision for overcoming the world is from the bottom-up through a radical kingdom ethic.

6. Newbigin, *The Gospel in a Pluralist Society*, 122.

Commanding Truths

"You have heard it said . . . But I say to you . . . "
(MATTHEW 5:21–22)

Eight beatitudes coupled with *you are* the salt and *you are* the light add up to a ten-fold description of the believer. Nothing has been earned or merited by our achievement or goodness. Everything is by grace—it has to be because of our sin and need. Matthew and Paul agree on this: "For it is by grace you have been saved, through faith—and this not from yourselves, it is the gift of God, not by works, so that no one can boast" (Ephesians 2:8-9). Seven commands follow in the sermon, just as good works follow for those created in Christ Jesus (Ephesians 2:10). The first command is to take the Word of God seriously. Jesus did not come to destroy but to fulfill the Law and the Prophets. "Jesus tells us how he feels about God's law before he delivers his exposition of that law at six salient points. A command to take God's law seriously is a command, too."[1]

The Sermon on the Mount's inclusiveness is countercultural. The Lord's commands are meant for all disciples. Our hierarchal habits of ranking and status seeking are swept aside. The Jesus way is the only way. There are no counsels of perfection ranked above the ordinary expectations of the followers of Jesus. There are no artificial distinctions between those who accept Jesus as Savior and those who accept him as Lord. We either follow Jesus as a member of his royal priesthood or we don't. There is not one standard for pastors and priests and another one for "simple" followers. There is no distinction between "believer" and "disciple."

The personal and practical impact of the Sermon on the Mount is also counter-cultural. "Modern enlightened culture is very theory-oriented," writes Charles Taylor. "We tend to live in our heads, trusting our disengaged understandings: of experience, of beauty, even the ethical."[2] The values of the secular age, such as tolerance, consent, mutual benefit, human rights, freedom, human flourishing, democracy, and equality, are abstract ideals that find their source in the self. The modern moral order is self-authorizing and self-authenticating. Society is made up of self-actualizing individuals held together by

1. Bruner, *The Churchbook: Matthew*, 1:196.
2. Taylor, *A Secular Age*, 555.

the "sociability of strangers."[3] Taylor calls this phenomenon *excarnation* (the opposite of incarnation). Instead
of embodied truth, enfleshed in forms of character and
action, we live in our heads. The excarnated ideals of the
modern moral order are framed as immanent abstract
ideals in a society of strangers each free to do their own
thing.

Jesus' description of beatitude-based obedience,
the kind that surpasses the righteousness of the scribes
and Pharisees, focuses on our relationship to others.
All seven commands relate to people. Anger, lust, and
divorce tend to deal with close personal relationships
whereas oaths, revenge, and hate have more to do with
societal relations. The source of these commands are
not grounded in the isolated, buffered self, but in the
will of God and since we are created in God's image they
have a resonance with our being that is innate within
us. Nevertheless, it is difficult for even the most sincere
believer to understand how he or she is being shaped by
the surrounding (secular) culture. The impact of "the
social imaginary," that subterranean reality that often
evades our conscious attention, is "much broader and
deeper than the intellectual schemes people may enter-
tain when they think about social reality in a disengaged
mode."[4] We are far more secular than we could ever

3. Taylor, *A Secular Age*, 575.
4. Taylor, *A Secular Age*, 171.

imagine, because the way we imagine the world is secular, not Christian. Jamie Smith explains, "This disembedded, buffered, individualistic view of the self seeps into our social imaginary—into the very way that we imagine the world, well before we ever think reflectively about it."[5]

The seven commands given by Jesus illustrate the greater righteousness and the fulfillment of the law. This is the righteousness that surpasses the righteousness of the Pharisees and the teachers of the law. These commands are set in contrast to the prevailing interpretation of the law. The tension between, "You have heard it said," and "But I say to you," distinguishes external compliance with the law (excarnational) with an internal embrace of the will of God (incarnational). In the secular age, "You have heard it said," may refer to a plethora of voices, a myriad of opinions, ideals, and ideologies. The "galloping pluralism" of the secular age bombards the person with customized options. The secular predisposition is all about the self. Commitment to others is for the sake of the self, so that we feel good about ourselves.

Social analyst Daniel Yankelovich writes, "By concentrating day and night on your feelings, potentials, needs, and wants, and desires, and by learning to assert them more freely, you do not become a freer, more spontaneous, more creative self; you become a narrower,

5. Smith, *How (Not) to Be Secular*, 45.

more self-centered, more isolated one. You do not grow, you shrink."[6] Although the external code of conduct may come in many forms they are all voices and opinions from the world that must be set over and against the will of God. This is easier said than done.

When C. S. Lewis became a Christian he described himself as being "at cross-purposes with the modern world. I have been a converted Pagan living among apostate Puritans."[7] James D. Hunter in *To Change the World* observes that many Christians who think that they are "on fire for Jesus" have no idea how they are influenced by the world. They see themselves as world-changers but in reality they are products of the world. Our veneer of cultural Christianity is no match for interfacing with the culture. Tim Keller writes, "It is a mistake to think that faithful believers in our time are not profoundly shaped by the narratives of modernity. We certainly are, and so when you unveil these narratives and interact with them in the ordinary course of preaching the Word, you help them see where they themselves may be more influenced by their society than by the Scripture, and

6. Daniel Yankelovich, *New Rules: Searching for Self-Fulfillment in a World Turned Upside Down* (New York: Bantam, 1981), 239.

7. C. S. Lewis, *Surprised by Joy* (London: Fontana, 1972), 60.

you give them important ways of communicating their faith to others."[8]

J. D. Vance in *Hillbilly Elegy: A Memoir of a Family and Culture in Crisis* provides an insightful and sobering account of entrenched enculturation. He writes, "I want people to understand that the demons of the life we left behind continue to chase us."[9] What made his childhood and future grim was a litany of everyday experiences endured by millions of Americans who live in Greater Appalachia and in the Post-Industrial Midwest and in the Deep South: bad public schools, an epidemic of pre-scription drug addition, a distorted work ethic, racism, sexism, folk religion, patterns of deception and manip-ulation, resentment, broken families, physical and sex-ual abuse, coarse, vulgar language, fierce family loyalty, unhealthy eating habits, and a systemic culture of blame, low expectations and excuses.

The loving loyalty of his grandparents and sister gave J. D. something to live for, but it was the Marines who gave him an identity and helped him to grow up. If he had learned helplessness and resentment at home, the Ma-rines turned him around and gave him a sense of self-re-spect, purpose, and confidence. He credits the Marines

8. Timothy Keller, *Preaching: Communicating Faith in an Age of Skepticism* (New York: Penguin, 2016), 118.

9. J. D. Vance, *Hillbilly Elegy: A Memoir of a Family and Culture in Crisis* (New York: Harper, 2018), 2.

with excising the feeling that his choices didn't matter. The Marines assumed "maximum ignorance from its enlisted folks" and then proceeded to teach them everything the Marine Corps thought they needed to know. They taught him that giving it your all was a way of life.

Deeply entrenched cultural habits get in the way of Jesus' real-world, down-to-earth obedience.

Jamie Smith in *Desiring the Kingdom* writes, "What if the rather abstract formulas of a Christian worldview turn out to be a way to tame and blunt the radical call to be a disciple of the coming kingdom? Could it be the case that learning a Christian perspective doesn't actually touch my desire, and that while I might be able to *think* about the world from a Christian perspective, at the end of the day I *love* not the kingdom of God but rather the kingdom of the market?"[10] Søren Kierkegaard put it this way, "Worldly wisdom is very willing to deceive by answering correctly the question, 'where is the road?' while life's true task is omitted, that is, how one walks along the road."[11]

The seven commands begin with the authority of the word and will of God. Jesus was accused of abolishing

---

10. James K. A. Smith, *Desiring the Kingdom: Worship, Worldview, and Cultural Formation* (Grand Rapids, MI: Baker, 2009), 218.

11. Søren Kierkegaard, *Provocations: Spiritual Writings of Kierkegaard*, ed. Charles E. Moore (Farmington, PA: The Plough Publishing House, 1999), 57.

the law, but nothing could be further from the truth. He came not to abolish, but to fulfill the law. Grace-grounded, beatitude-based believers live daily in the dynamic synergy of law and gospel precisely because they are justified by faith, not by works. The law that was over and against us has been transformed by the gospel into a law that is for us. "The law of God sends us to Christ for salvation—to be justified; and Christ sends us back to the law to be sanctified."[12] There is no conflict between the law and gospel. "There is no need for the law to pass away, in order to establish the gospel—both agree perfectly.... The gospel being no other than the commands of the law, proposed by way of promise." For Wesley, when the law of God is viewed in the light of the gospel it is filled with "great and precious promises."[13]

In the Sermon on the Mount Jesus addresses the sanctity of life, the meaning of love, the fidelity of marriage, the necessity of truthfulness, the costly commitment to justice, and the power of loving your enemy. We could spend hours and hours on each of these subjects, and we do because we must, but it is good for us to recognize that Jesus summed up his kingdom ethic in a concise five minute synopsis. No one gets lost in the rhetoric as

12. John R. W. Stott, *The Sermon on the Mount* (Downers Grove, IL: IVP, 1985), 120.

13. John Wesley, *Wesley's Works: Sermon on the Mount*, vol. 5 (London: Wesleyan Conference Office, 1878), 5:313.

Jesus goes to the heart of heart righteousness. The scope of Jesus' kingdom ethic shapes the self in relationship to society in ways that strengthen the person-in-community. Instead of an external code, Jesus lays out a visible righteousness that comes from the heart.

For the Pharisees the law outlawed murder, regulated sex and marriage, and laid down rules for telling the truth, achieving justice, and dealing with your enemies. For Jesus the law of God outlawed anger, honored the beauty of sex and marriage, and made truthfulness, justice, and love the hallmarks of his kingdom ethic. The difference between the Pharisees and Jesus was the difference between laying down the law for a group of prison inmates and living out the law of love in a family and in society. In prison the goal is to keep the inmates from hurting one another. In a family the goal is to show love to one another.

The difference between the first century's nuanced religious compliance with the law and the plethora of perspectives in the secular age is the "self." The late modern phenomenon of the imperial self stands in place of the law and over and against God. In theory much is said about human rights and tolerance but there is no moral foundation for saying it is wrong to hate my brother or disparage my sister. The secular age replaces the beauty, purity, and fidelity of sex and the covenant of marriage with the notion of consensual sex. There is no higher purpose or meaning other than the satisfaction of the modern self's longings and desires.

Anthony Bourdain with his larger than life persona and his "everyman" celebrity status stands as an iconic figure in our late-modern Age of Authenticity. One of his colleagues said, "Everybody wants to be Anthony Bourdain, overliquored, overfed, traveling the world, having fun, connecting with people, and getting paid for it." Surprised that he survived his twenties, Bourdain wrestled with the demons of alcohol, heroin, and cocaine. He said, "I looked in the mirror and I saw somebody worth saving." Bourdain disabuses his followers of any deeper, transcendent meaning. He relishes the line, "Your body is not a temple, it's an amusement park. Enjoy the ride."[14]

Jesus might rephrase the line, "that unless your righteousness surpasses that of the Pharisees (the religious) you will not enter the kingdom of heaven," to say, "that unless your experience of human flourishing surpasses the flourishing of the self-satisfied person, you will never be fulfilled." The Jesus way defines human flourishing differently from the world. It includes self-denial and self-sacrifice. Charles Taylor writes, "There is a notion of our good which goes beyond human flourishing, which we may gain even while failing utterly on the scales of human flourishing, even through such a failing (like dying

---

14. Anthony Bourdain, *Kitchen Confidential* (New York: Ecco, 2007), 73.

young on a cross). . . . The paradox of Christianity . . . is that on the one hand, it seems to assert the unconditional benevolence of God . . . and yet it redefines our ends so as to take us beyond flourishing."[15] Jesus called for "unusual Christians in all the usual situations."[16] True obedience means love instead of hate, purity instead of lust, fidelity instead of infidelity, honesty instead of dishonesty, reconciliation instead of retaliation, and prayer instead of revenge.

15. Taylor, *A Secular Age*, 151.
16. Bruner, *The Churchbook: Matthew*, 1:206.

True Spirituality

"Be careful not to practice your righteousness in front of others to be seen by them." (MATTHEW 6:1)

Religion in the secular age is more likely to begin here, with the duty of religious practices, than it is to begin where Jesus began, with the heartfelt visible, social righteousness outlined in Matthew 5. This is because even in the secular age spiritual practices provide religious self-justification. To the religious they offer a way to measure religious sincerity. To the secularist, they provide important psychological and emotional coping strategies. This is why people say they are "spiritual" who have no interest in God. They are fine with prayer as a technique, a calming mental exercise, but Jesus saw the spiritual disciplines, not as coping strategies, but as the essential means by which we relate to our Father in heaven. The hidden righteousness of personal communion with God pushes back against the immanent frame of the secular age. True spirituality flies in the face of the malaise of immanence. Jamie Smith defines the immanent frame as "a constructed social space that frames our lives entirely within a natural (rather than supernatural) order. It is the circumscribed space of the modern social imaginary that precludes transcendence."[1]

Jesus uses the devotions—giving, praying, fasting—to set in contrast the small world of our making with the large world of God's saving. We pray, "Our Father in heaven, hallowed by your name, your kingdom come, your will be done, on earth as it is in heaven." In his novel *Saturday,* Ian McEwan captures the general ethos of the modern world-view through the eyes of Theo, an eighteen-year-old. Theo belongs to a "sincerely godless generation." "No one in his bright, plate-glass, forward-looking school ever asked him to pray, or sing an impenetrable cheery hymn. There's no entity [*like a loving, redeeming God*] for him to doubt. His initiation, in front of the TV, before the dissolving towers World Trade Center towers, was intense but he had adapted quickly."[2]

Theo has his own unique philosophy for coping with life, but it is really not a philosophy as much as an aphorism—a maxim. It's only a saying, not even a sentence, but it reduces everything down to a manageable size. Theo's advice is this: "the bigger you think, the crappier it looks." He explains, "When we go on about big things,

---

1. Smith, *How (Not) to Be Secular*, 141.
2. Ian McEwan, *Saturday* (New York: Knopf, 2006), 32.

the political situation, global warming, world poverty, it all looks really terrible, with nothing better, nothing to look forward to. But when I think small, closer in—you know, a girl I've just met . . . or snowboarding next month, then it looks great. So this is going to be my motto—think small."[3] Theo's coping strategy is typical of Western affluent people who have little to live for apart from the immediate moment. Theo limits his imagination out of fear, so as not to be overwhelmed by human tragedy.

God's truth becomes internalized and actualized through daily communion with God. This is how Jesus' kingdom ethic becomes embedded in our hearts and lives. "Tragedy will pulverize a subjective, individually crafted, emotion-based faith," writes Cameron Cole.[4] This is the kind of external religion that knows no personal (secret) communion with God. When Cameron suffered the lost of his three year old son he understood the significance of the truth that truly defined his self-identity—the embedded truth. He writes, "There are some truths that mean nothing to a person who is gasping for existential air. When tears seem to flow continuously in your life, the nuances of the Trinity or the particulars of a certain end-times theory do nothing to comfort. However, other biblical concepts can walk a person back off the meta-

3. McEwan, *Saturday*, 35.
4. Cameron Cole, *Therefore I Have Hope: 12 Truths That Comfort, Sustain, and Redeem in Tragedy* (Wheaton, IL: Crossway, 2018), 53.

phorical or literal ledge when jumping seems so reasonable and appealing. . . . One night I sat down and wrote down all of these comforting theological principles as a personal creed. I began to realize that the Lord had embedded these individual truths in my heart that collectively constructed a narrative under which I could live during my Worst. This narrative gave me hope."[5]

Beatitude-based character leads to salt and light impact. True heart righteousness produces visible, social righteousness. The guiding principle for visible righteousness is clear: "Let your light shine before people, that they may see your good deeds and praise your Father in heaven" (Matthew 5:16). But when it comes to the hidden righteousness of personal spirituality there is a clear and contrasting picture: "Be careful not to do your 'acts of righteousness' before people, to be seen by them. If you do, you will have no reward from your Father in heaven" (Matthew 6:1). On the one hand, Jesus is telling his disciples to "let your light shine." On the other, he is saying 'keep your acts of righteousness secret." Either Jesus changed his mind in the middle of his message or else he purposely confronted us with a paradox. There is a right way and a wrong way to be visible about our faith in Christ. There's a difference between the visible righteousness God intends the world to see and the hidden righteousness meant for only God to see. If we

5. Cole, *Therefore I Have Hope*, 18.

are not careful, giving, praying, and fasting can become a performance.

The most solid witness to authentic spirituality comes quietly and unobtrusively. Real giving, praying and fasting are not for others to see, but for God to receive. The practice of hidden righteousness is evident in the believer's quiet dependence upon God. This unflaunted, secret spirituality bears the true reward. The intimacy and significance of personal communion with God brings about the desired end. Taking up the easy yoke liberates us from pretense and performance. Hidden righteousness turns religion into relationship and ritual into worship. We no longer feel strange and foreign in God's presence. We are there, not out of duty or for the approval of others, but out of our love for God in Christ. Publicity and promotion only serve to distract from the real work at hand: "to know Christ and the power of his resurrection and the fellowship of sharing in his sufferings, becoming like him in his death" (Philippians 3:10).

Liberating Constraints

"Do not store up for yourselves treasures on earth."
(MATTHEW 6:19)

Jesus spells out the prohibitions that liberate. As he draws his sermon to a conclusion he fires off a series of blunt staccato statements that leave no doubt as to his spiritual direction when it comes to the values, vision, and loyalty of the believing community. Jesus' dos and don'ts are very different from the selective check-list that many Christians experience and seek to practice. Jesus' list shuns legalism and avoids the moralistic quick fix. Obedience is not a matter of appearances. Jesus insists on going to the heart of the matter, and severing the tie that binds our souls to the ways of the world. "Do not store up for yourselves treasures on earth.... Do not serve two masters.... Do not worry about your life.... Do not judge others.... Do not give to dogs what is sacred." These are the negatives that free us to be positive. If we don't get these "no's" down, we'll never know the positive "yes" of God's life in us. Today's laid-back, easy-going, connect-the-dots, paint-by-number Christianity, on sale everywhere, is not found in the Sermon on the Mount.

In Matthew 6:25-7:12 Jesus identifies four sometimes subtle, but always stubborn, forms of spiritual *distortion*: excessive worry, divided loyalties, judgmental criticism, and forced evangelism. Contrary to popular opinion, these activities do not build up the Body of Christ, they wear it out. Many labor under a false expectation of what is required of them. They succumb to internal and external religious pressure that needlessly increase the burden of the Christian life. They are subtle because they are cloaked in righteousness. They are dangerous, because when they are yielded to, they ruin our walk with Christ. If we are serious about following Jesus we will want to watch out for these false expectations and pressures.

None of Jesus' prohibitions are surprising. They are consistent with what it means to be beatitude-based believers with salt and light impact. What Jesus says here has already been said. But we need to be told again and again so that the persuasive power of the culture is overcome and these truths are embedded in our souls and daily practices. Some believers struggle with the decisiveness of Jesus' spiritual direction. We prefer to keep our options open. We want our treasures on earth and in heaven and we're just fine serving two masters. The problem is that Jesus didn't offer these compromising options. He calls for total obedience and exclusive loyalty. Every day is a choice between ambitions, visions, and masters—and every day Jesus should win.

Writer David Brooks began his 2015 commencement address at Dartmouth by cutting out, as he said, "the usual garbage advice" of commencement speakers, like "Listen to your inner voice. Be true to yourself. Follow your passion. Your future is limitless. Don't be afraid to fail." He titled his address "The Ultimate Spoiler Alert" and gave the graduates a picture of their life to come. He talked about the long hard search for a job. He promised that their 20s would be one of the happiest phases of life, but that there would be long periods of loneliness and heartbreak. Brooks encouraged the graduates that through trial and error they would discover their true loves and come up with their own criteria for success.

"By the time you hit your 30s, you will realize that your primary mission in life is to be really good at making commitments." "Making a commitment," Brooks says, "simply means falling in love with something and then building a structure of behavior around it that will carry you through when your love falters." He outlined four key commitments: to your spouse and family; to your career and vocation; to your faith or philosophy; to your community and village."

Real love operates on two levels, "the level of gritty reality and the level of transcendent magic." Love takes you out of yourself. It casts off cost-benefit analysis. Love demands that you enter into a different and inverse logic. It is self-sacrificing; it is self-denying for the sake of the other. Love defies normal utilitarian logic. Love calls for moral logic. You have to conquer your desire to get what you crave. You have to make commitments. "Adulthood is about closing around commitments. Dartmouth has opened your mind. The purpose of an open mind is to close around certain beliefs. The highest joy is found in sending down roots." Brooks hoped the grads would look back over the totality of their lives and experience a sense of gratitude for a life filled with joy, "a joy beyond anything they could possibly have earned."[1]

Brooks' commencement address is beautiful, filled with uncommon, common grace. He is winsome and witty, a gracious, hopeful advocate for the moral order. He is all for taming the self-centered, selfish self, and he is all for living into life-long commitments. But I can't shake the nagging thought that sensible types like David Brooks pose a real threat to the gospel. Brooks believes in everything reasonable, everything, that is, but the stuff our culture calls weird. He avoids all the absurdities, like the Virgin Birth, the Incarnation, the Atoning Sacrifice of Christ on the Cross, the bodily Resurrection and the Ascension. Brooks never identifies the source for his

1. David Brooks, "The Ultimate Spoiler Alert," commencement address, Dartmouth College, June 14, 2015.

uncommon common grace. This is wisdom without the beatitudes, without sin and salvation, without God in Christ reconciling the world unto himself. This is the wisdom of self-acceptance over forgiveness, and affirmation over atonement. This is the wisdom without the love of the Father, the grace of the Son, and the fellowship of the Holy Spirit.

Brooks represents the sensible, modern wisdom that caused the Danish Christian thinker Søren Kierkegaard to identify the great invisible truths of the gospel as *Absurd*: "Christianity has declared itself to be the eternal essential truth which has come into being in time. . . . It has required of the individual the inwardness of faith in relation to that which is an offense to the Jews and folly to the Greeks—and an absurdity to understanding."[2] This is why the world thinks Christians are weird, and who can blame them? Of course the world thinks the followers of Jesus are strange. The gospel speaks of truths the world finds utterly inexplicable. T. S. Eliot observed in the 1930s: "The World is trying the experiment of attempting to form a civilized but non-Christian mentality. The experiment will fail; but we must be very patient in awaiting its collapse; meanwhile redeeming the time: so that the Faith may be preserved alive through the dark

2. Robert Bretall, ed., *A Kierkegaard Anthology* (New York: The Modern Library, 1958), 222.

ages before us; to renew and rebuild civilization, and save the World from suicide."[3]

There is an amazing aplomb among late modern thinkers who conclude that life is absurd, even pointless, but cling tenaciously to a positive attitude toward life. Writer Barbara Ehrenreich reasons, "You can think of death bitterly or with resignation, as a tragic interruption of your life, and take every possible measure to postpone it. Or, more realistically, you can think of life as an interruption of an eternity of personal nonexistence, and seize it as a brief opportunity to observe and interact with the living, ever-surprising world around us."[4]

Facing the fact that there is no transcendent meaning to life is no different than being told that death ends all. It is surely harder to believe in the gospel if you have come to believe that there is no grand narrative, that there is only your own little story that is truer to the chaos and disorder of the universe. This leaves us with nothing, but a self-centered existence. By default, I get lost in the abstract argument in my head "day in day out," knowing that it falls to me to create meaning and to decide what

3. Quoted in Jeremiah Webster, *Paradise in The Waste Land* (Milwaukee, WI: Wiseblood Books, 2013), 11.

4. Barbara Ehrenreich, *Natural Causes: An Epidemic of Wellness, the Certainty of Dying, and Killing Ourselves to Live Longer* (New York: Twelve, 2018), xv.

to worship.[5] "The freedom to be lords of our tiny skull-sized kingdoms, alone at the center of all creation," does not compare, argues David Foster Wallace, to the really important "freedom that involves attention and awareness and discipline, and being able truly to care about other people and to sacrifice for them over and over in myriad petty, unsexy ways every day." For Wallace "the capital-T Truth is about life *before* death" (emphasis his). It is about "simple awareness" of what "is so real and essential, so hidden in plain sight all around us." And perhaps this indeed is the best we can do if there is no triune God who gave us his blessing in person.

5. David Foster Wallace, "This Is Water," 2005 Kenyon Commencement address, https://fs.blog/2012/04/david-foster-wallace-this-is-water/.

Decisive Imperatives

"Enter through the narrow gate." (MATTHEW 7:13)

Jesus began with beatitudes, not demands. He ends with imperatives. Modern sermons have a way of easing us out the door into the virtual reality of business as usual. Jesus does the opposite. He forces the issue. He cuts through whatever ambiguity may arise and calls for a decision. Jesus weaves his conclusion with metaphors (gates, sheep and wolves, fruit trees, and storms) to stress a single meaning. The conclusion of the Sermon calls us to act wisely because there are extraordinary consequences to our actions. We can choose the right path or the wrong path. We can lay the right foundation or the wrong one. Jesus would be remiss if he did not warn us that the responsibility to choose wisely, discern carefully, and act faithfully, was ours and ours alone. But as we have seen throughout the sermon, the decision to act is framed by transcendent meaning, the revelation of God in Christ and the meta-narrative of salvation history. The gospel has given us a plausibility structure, one that is not shared by the world. Leslie Newbigin wrote, "It is no secret, indeed it has been affirmed from the beginning, that the gospel gives rise to a new plausibility structure, a radically different vision of things from those that shape all human cultures apart from the gospel. The Church, therefore, as the bearer of the gospel, inhabits a plausibility structure which is at variance with, and which calls in question, those that govern all human cultures without exception."[1]

Nothing is said or implied here to ease the burden of choosing the Jesus way. Not even that God promises to guide and empower us to do the right thing. No mention is made here of the Holy Spirit guiding our path-finding, quickening our decision-making, empowering our truth-discerning obedience, even though we know this to be absolutely true. The light burden of the easy yoke does not remove from our shoulders the responsibility to discern who is telling the truth and who is a wolf in sheep's clothing.

Jesus concludes with three warnings: "Enter through the narrow gate." "Watch out for false prophets." "Don't build your house on the sand." The three warnings cor-

1. Newbigin, *The Gospel in a Pluralistic Society*, 9.

respond to the testimony of Jesus: "I am the way and the truth and the life. No one comes to the Father except through me" (John 14:6). The way is the narrow gate; the truth is discerning false prophets; the life is building on the rock instead of sand. These three warnings focus on the difference between external appearance and internal reality. It is as if Jesus is saying don't be fooled. There is a greater righteousness, a heart righteousness, that surpasses the righteousness of the scribes and Pharisees. The issue is between internal versus external righteousness "that has marked the entirety of the Sermon."[2] Hagner writes, "...The essence of discipleship...is found not in words, nor in religiosity, nor even in performance of spectacular deeds in the name of Jesus, but only in the manifestation of true righteousness—doing the will of the Father as now interpreted through the teaching of Jesus."[3] We face a choice between two ways that are radically different but appearances are deceptive. Broadway is appealing, false prophets are dressed in sheep's cloth-

2. Jonathan Pennington, *The Sermon on the Mount and Human Flourishing: A Theological Commentary* (Grand Rapids, MI: Baker, 2018), 273.

3. Donald Hagner, *Word Biblical Commentary: Matthew 1-13* (Grand Rapids, MI: Zondervan, 2017), 188.

ing, outwardly righteous types can perform miraculous deeds, and a fine home can be built on sand.

Missionary statesman E. Stanley Jones boiled the options down to choosing between the cult of self expression and the calling of Christ to self-denial. Jones wrote in 1931, "There are just two great philosophies of life. Nietzsche summed up the one way when he said: 'Assert yourself. Care for nothing except for yourself. Be strong, be a superman. The world is yours if you can get it.' Here is the cult of self-expression. . . . it is ruthless in Nietzsche; it is refined in others." Jones explained the second option: "Jesus stands as the utter opposite of that, and says that the way to find life is to lose it, that the way of self-realization is by the way of self-renunciation. He says: 'If anyone would come after me, let them deny themselves (literally 'utterly reject'), and take up their cross and follow me.' No two ways could be more opposed."[4]

We might like an indecisive "maybe," the kind of middle-of-the road Christianity that is all too common today. But what Jesus gives us instead are stark *either/or* alternatives: two ways (broad and narrow), two teachers (false and true), and finally two foundations (sand and rock). The Sermon on the Mount ends with a parable about two kinds of builders: one who builds on the rock and one who builds on the sand. The difference

4. Jones, *The Christ of the Mount*, 45.

between them comes down to hearing the words of Jesus and putting them into practice. The contrast is between Jesus, who is the way, the truth, and the life, and the alternative path, the way of the world. Everything depends upon hearing the word of the Lord and doing it. "For the doctrine is indeed good and excellent," concluded Luther, "but it is not preached in order to be heard, it is preached to be applied to practical life."[5] Dietrich Bonhoeffer offers a similar conviction when he writes, "Humanly speaking, we could understand and interpret the Sermon on the Mount in a thousand different ways. Jesus knows only one possibility: simple surrender and obedience, not interpreting it or applying it, but doing and obeying it. That is the only way to hear his word."[6]

The metaphor of the rock invites us to consider Jesus' dialogue with the disciples in Matthew 16. Jesus Christ is the Master of the house. He is the Christ, the Son of the living God, and on this rock he builds his church and the gates of hell will not overcome it (Matthew 16:18). We cannot domesticate the gospel to fit the plausibility structures of the late modern mind. We believe that the gospel of Jesus Christ is true for everyone everywhere. We invite people to stand with us on the

5. Martin Luther, *Commentary on Sermon on the Mount* (Bellingham, WA: Lexham Press, 2017), 322.

6. Dietrich Bonhoeffer, *The Cost of Discipleship* (New York: Macmillan, 1966), 218–19.

rock and to become beatitude-based believers—to become the people of God with salt and light impact, who practice heart-righteousness, faithful obedience, true spirituality, and genuine freedom amidst the pressures of the world.

Questions for Reflection and Discussion

1. Why did Jesus give the Sermon on the Mount?
2. What does it mean to be a beatitude-based believer?
3. What gives the Sermon its cross-cultural appeal and its counter-cultural impact?
4. Compare the cultural voices in your experience ("You heard it said...") and the voice of Christ ("But I say to you...").
5. Which of the "commands" stands out to you?
6. Why did Jesus begin with the social impact of the gospel before teaching on giving, praying, fasting?
7. How are the "do nots" different from the "do nots" that many Christians grow up with?
8. What makes these "do nots" both liberating and difficult?
9. Where is the grace of Christ in the demanding imperatives that conclude the Sermon?
10. How does Jesus' authority differ from secular and religious authorities today?